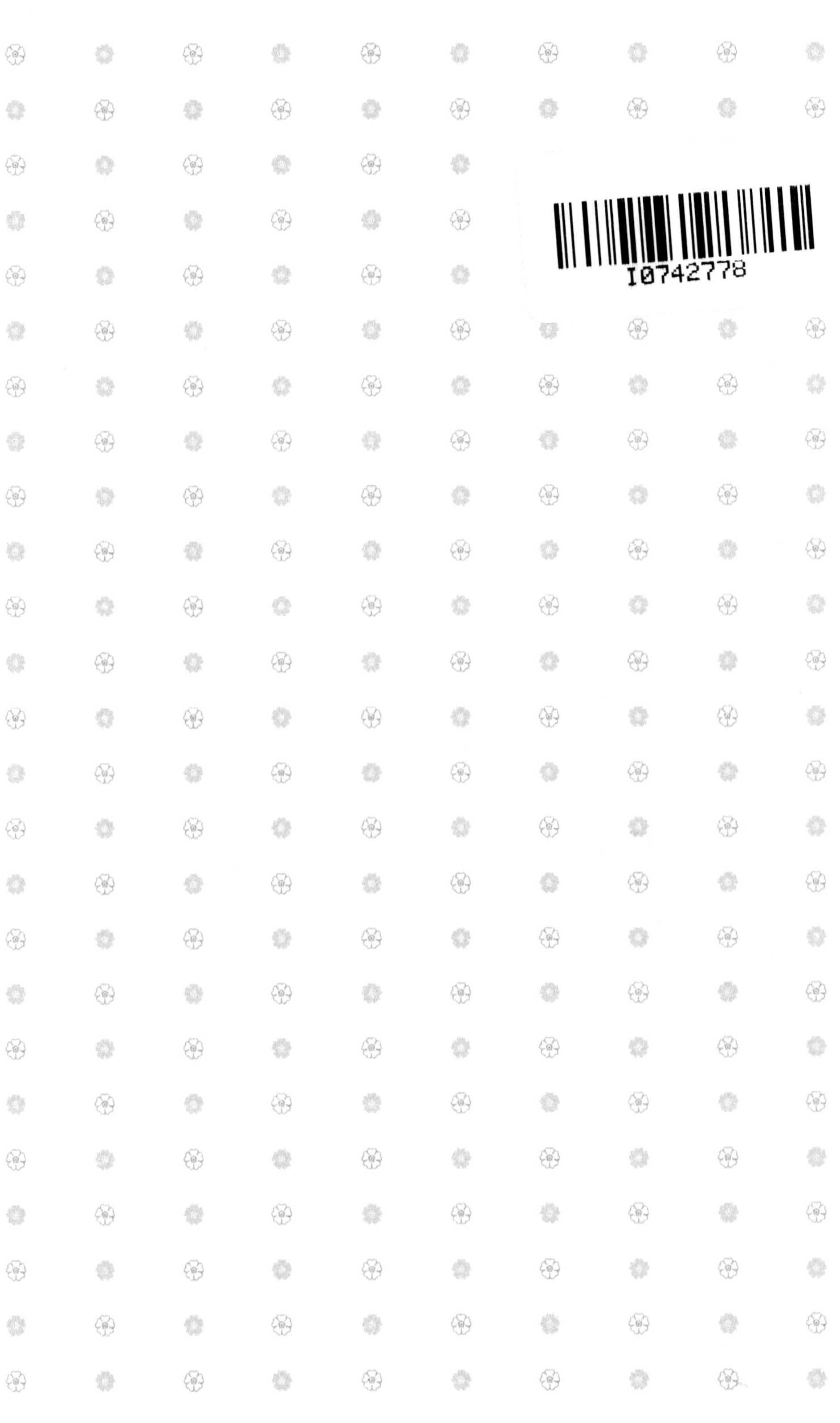
I0742778

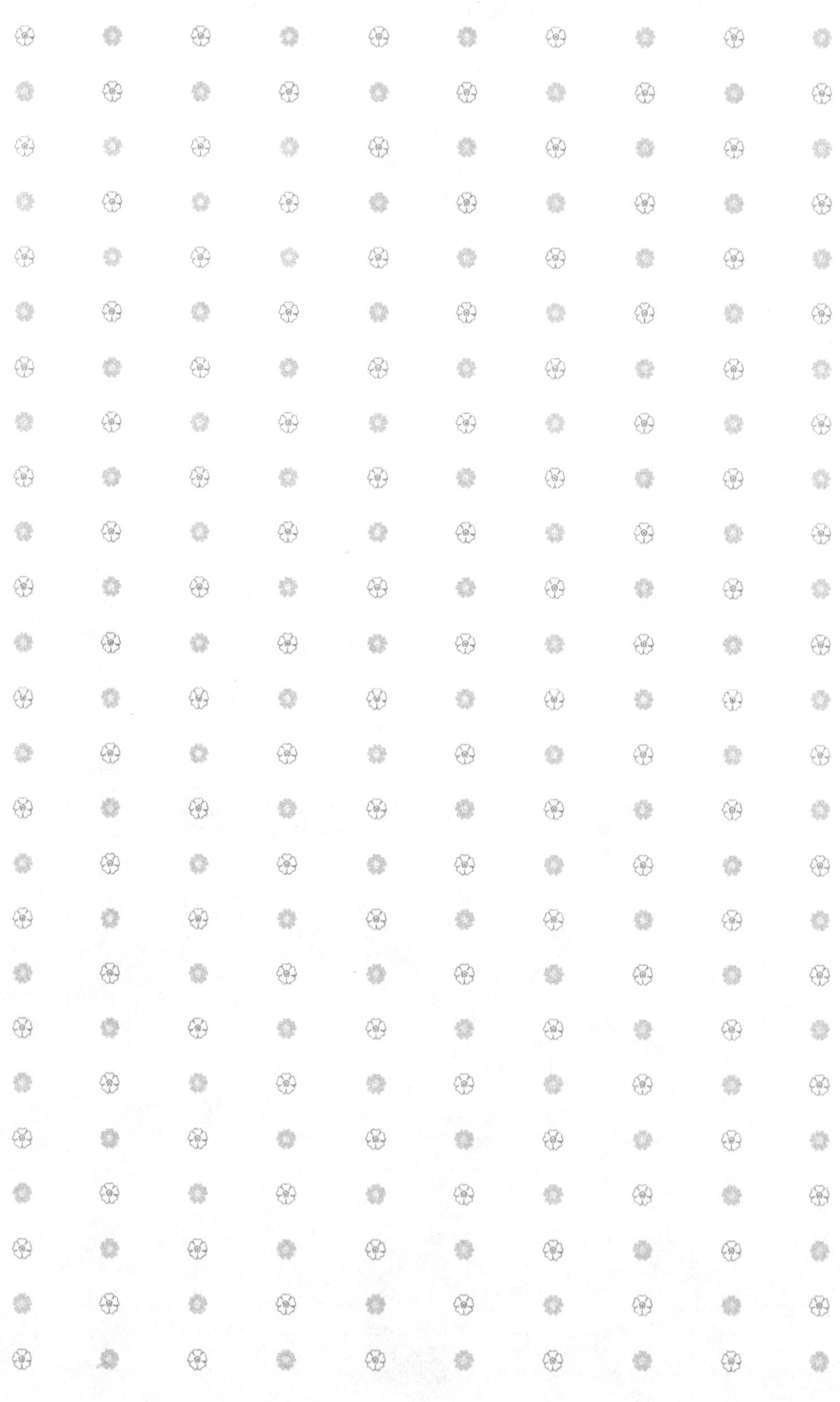

in case of emergency press

We are proud to acknowledge the Traditional Owners of
country throughout Australia and to recognise their
continuing connection to land, waters, and culture.
We pay our respects to their Elders.

We support recognition, reconciliation, and reparation.

The Crow on the Cross

Wedding Songs & Others

Steve Evans

in case of emergency press
https://icoe.com.au
Travancore, Victoria
Australia

Published by in case of emergency press 2024

ISBN: 978-0-6486111-1-0

Cover design: Brad Horawry

Cover image: 'Crow Silhouetted on Cross - Anglican Church - Tsigehtchic - Near Inuvik - Northwest Territories – Canada'
by Dr. Adam Jones

Acknowledgements

Poems in this selection, or earlier versions of them, have appeared in *Another Universe, Beyond the Shimmering, Blur, The Canberra Times, Divan, Fleurieu Flow, Fluorescent Voices, Friendly Street Anthology No. 46 & 48, Friendly Street Poets Poem of the Month* (December 2022 and July 2023), *Kaleidoscope, Light and Glorie, The Montreal Poetry Prize Anthology 2022, New England Review, Poetry Scotland, Pure Slush: Marriage – Life Span No. 6, Social Alternatives, Storm Anthology – Minds Shine Bright, Unruly Sun, Viewpoint, War Music and Other Poems,* and *Westerly.*

Author's note

These poems and the characters represented in them are fictions, although some scenarios and issues relate to experiences that people might encounter in real life, for better or worse.

This work was written on the unceded lands of the Kaurna people. The author acknowledges them as the traditional custodians and pays respects to their ancestors and Elders, past and present, as well as their unique cultural and spiritual relationships to the land, waters and seas, and their rich contribution to society.

Dedication

To my father
Stephen Douglas 'Doug' Evans

Table of Contents

The Crow on the Cross

Wedding Songs & Others

Poems by Steve Evans

A Book of Wedding Songs

The Crow on the Cross

From the steeple cross
I see the glossed white tin
of your bridal car approaching.
I adjust tail feathers the lustre of coal.
A porcelain sheen turns on my wings
deep as black water.

I alight from the spire in a lazy arc,
step into church with my coat ablaze.
Was there ever as sleek a groom?
Was there ever a sharper foil for a bride
than this lit darkness,
this brilliance I am?

My beak is full of spells,
a gush of wedding song.
I will sing the fractured axis.
I will sing the ghost of longing.
I will sing the wild tilt of unearthed things
and pour us back into the sky.
We will fly,
bird and bride,
with all the angled winds
a riff on the bible of flight.

See,
your plumage already begins to grow.
Come with me.
Leave your long white car.
Leave your grieving family.

The mouth of death won't have us yet.
Let them look for us in skies and trees.
We will look back from the little cross.
We will peer through the stained glass
and sing our inelegant tunes,
the hymns to loss and faith,
the long, wet light of winter on us.

Bridal Waltz

I am up late
> marking students' papers
when you enter the room
> in your wedding gown.
It is beautiful on you still,
> a bit snug now
but you are under sail
> all style and cleavage.

Maybe enchanted
> or maybe under the
humour of its elegant
> and regal presence,
you decide to wear it
> all the next day—
on the train to work
> and interviewing clients,
on your lunchtime walk,
> and shopping for lunch.
You carve a path of calm
> in the frenzy of the city.

By the time you get home
> I am feeling foolish,
with flowers, in my suit
> and waiting on bended knee.
The choir of neighbourhood kids
> seems a bit redundant
and my little speech silly,
> especially when you say
you've already received
> three proposals that day.

Finally, in the house alone,
    we hang up the suit and gown,
those ghostly chaperones,
    and begin the dance
of the newlyweds,
    naked, blessed.

Prenuptial

She handed me the papers.
Just sign
here
  and here.
Now promise to wed in mystery,
to fight in perfect harmony.

Don't ask what I do
for a living.
If I'm gone for a while
don't expect postcards.
You can me write me love letters
but I won't read them.

Now take my clothes off
slowly
and kiss me—
here
  and here.

The Burning River

On my last New Year's Eve in the town
after the parties all died down,
Cowley's mob stole a petrol drum
to set the water alight
and where we had earlier swum
tipping our mouths back wide
in that soft confluence of river and summer rain
was a wild rag of blue flame
that I watched from the jetty,
the burning river a signal to the stars
and those about to leave this place.
But now my feet leave no prints on that soft shore,
the lights of town squint to a blur
and I sweep from here to anywhere
as easy as flicking stations
on the Falcon's radio—
invisible.

I slide past the open shed at the corner sawmill.
The stacked sap-wet ends of new timber
are raw 45s with the years' slow music in their rings.
Blonde stalagmites of dust lie under the bench
where Tom Wright lost a finger
to a second's dreaming
and when asked how he did it,
absently showed them with another one.

At town's edge
cattle like scattered handbags
still graze the hillside above Baxter's dump
where heaped papers in constant migration
churn through summer air

and accidental sculptures of cast-out wire
lie tangled as my old homework excuses.
A broken pram on its side
is a billycart in waiting
and the gold and orange
of nasturtiums along the road
will work their mysteries of light
in morning's glare.

I pass the paddock's charred circle
where we jumped at Guy Fawkes' crackers,
those rattling little ladders of red and green,
the strings of squibs thrashing underfoot,
and where the tang of soursobs in spring
was as bitter as old torch batteries
tested on the tongue.
Now thistles' cardboard crowns crowd along the fence,
and the flat ground has been graded into squares,
a dusty map for new houses
that are still a long time coming.

In Newland Road,
in that house with worn shutters,
I am nine years old,
sprawled across a soft-sprung bed
dreaming of the fastest bicycle in the world,
half-pedalling it already,
my mother by the kitchen radio
re-stitching collars on my father's shirts
and he two days away
on a sales round through
other towns just like this one.

At Pattersons' place down our street,
the dog's dish is an old hubcap,
their side-gate's an ancient iron bedstead.

Chooks in the their doorless fridge out back
are tucked into crooning sleep
quieter than the Patterson twins
who snore on the cool of the veranda floor.
Mick Junior chasing sparrows
with a pinch of salt
can't even catch them in sleep's fantasies.

Heather Timms.
Heather Timms.
What became of Heather Timms?
The gossips said she left a note,
that she eloped at seventeen.
She fell into the dark.
I wondered about weddings
and missed her.
Her absence hung about us.
Her mother left town.
Her father would not speak
though I knocked on her door for weeks.

The streets I ran
are quiet now in night's held breath
but all of yesterday's scraps revolve,
the brash colours and faces flashing their instant
like summer slideshows in the garden,
images floating on a hung white sheet,
every time I step out
dreaming my old town.

And Yes

What can one say to newlyweds
that doesn't involve a sweet retreat
to primal pleasures?
Here are the inevitable lines
alluding to the beauty of a sky
that brims with nothing but blue,
or a river of stars.
There is the conjured gaze of love,
a painted portrait of the serene couple.
Always this temptation to resort to poor replicas.

We could wheel out the box of familiar parts,
reaching into drawers named Trust and Devotion
but they are always empty.
That work's an illusion.
No-one has seen such insubstantial objects.
They do not live in boxes.

Let's not wave old flags
but share the joy of the inexpressible,
and think of these two
standing in a space beyond words
where they have joined hands,
together at the crossing point.

What can one ever say to newlyweds
after this
but Yes
and Yes?

White (1)

in the National Gallery of Victoria

That itch of white
starts at me when I first walk in.
The tablecloth in McCubbin's 'Sketch for After Breakfast'.
Then dirty washing over there,
its afternoon glare,
and a cloud blowing overhead
is blown twice.
Once in the sky.
Its twin on the water is sunlit too,
bright as sand arcing at the edge
of the next picture's lake,
a saucer's rim
where bleached shells tipped onto the beach
are broken china
ground into flakes of meringue
stark as a wedding dress,
a starched apron hung on the line
beneath a white moon in a white sky.
The tablecloth gave it to the clouds
that flung it back.
The lake washed it clean and threw its milky
light into buckling shifts of sky.

I'm pulled from frame to frame by all these
snatches of white until I have to
shade my eyes and duck my head—
everything one
and blinding.

Postmodern

The bride wanted horses and coach
but inside the church
already an uproar of pipe-organ
and Uncle Henry pinching the bridesmaids
vows made never to resort
to innuendo and smutty
jokes in drunken speeches
before confetti flickers on the aisle
with Dad's relief that finally
the gowned one has arrived
as he's sent out to get the groom
whose tie's crooked from the slap he copped
when one last feel tickled no fancy
and you a nearly married man
have you no shame
now get in there and do the right thing
before someone discovers you
then an alcoholic accordion and
club-footed piano crank out
the waltz to announce
a honeymoon suitcase parked
by the door of the graffiti'd car
that's already gone.
We won't be trying this again soon.

White (2)

The cool surface of scalded cream
left under a lace doily
on the dawn veranda.

The curtain dazzling
when daylight's slow tide
fills the room.

The stilled wheels of dinner plates,
a row of white port holes
standing on the shelf.

Finding you in the hallway
wearing your wedding dress
and a fold of afternoon sun.

The ivory of wax
in the hive
long before the wick is lit.

The candle stuttering in our room,
trying over and over
to describe you.

An Audience with Julie

having borrowed his best friend's bike and his older
brother's suit he took a day off driving trucks came down
to where she worked wedged a bunch of stolen flowers
against the bars that arrived almost intact and he had to
tell the gateman his plan or they wouldn't let him into
Preston's clothing factory even with his flowers and suit

his heart light with the thrill and fear too nervous for
rehearsals he'd have to wait to hear the words that he
would offer when he found her there and as he passed the
rows of girls all their machines fell silent while a wash of
murmurs pushed him on

he knew someone had told her from the way she turned
her head as chafe-necked and suit-awkward he
approached her while the sewing team looked at her not
him as he said his weeks were fifty hours with the overtime
and next year he'd make foreman if one more shift came on
and they'd rent a place the first year while they saved to
buy their own

and could she, that is, if he, maybe, would she, anyway...?
and the knock-off whistle screamed so when her hands
went to her face he couldn't hear her say a thing and in the
quiet that came next a hundred women watched her and
Julie did not speak though all the floor held tight its breath

he left the flowers on the roadside hung his brother's suit
back up drove the trucks and slept between shifts as if he
didn't care though he'd turn that puzzle over in his mind
for years and years the terrible beauty of a late afternoon
in the western suburbs that bicycle still shining and a
hundred lookers-on and how a red-haired girl who loved
him could say no without a sound

Always

A woman in a wedding dress
takes tickets on the tram.
Her hem is scuffed and dirty,
mouth fixed as a post-box slot.
Another one cutting ham
in the corner shop
throws back her fly-wire veil—
next order please!

Others scrunched in car seats
sitting at red lights
bustle in a mass of tulle,
tap unringed fingers on their wheels.
The mechanics and plumbers,
the clerks and sales assistants
in a froth of silk,
the dentists and cleaners
in hand-stitched satin trains—
the army of them waiting
in their vast white uniforms
ready at a moment's notice
but always the bridesmaid
never the bride.

Until the bonfires,
the great gatherings in parks
and at beaches,
where their faces are lit by
the upward-sweeping flames
fed by dress after dress
as they are sung
into the farewell sparks and stars.

Haute Couture

The salesman's scowl says it all—
billowing falls of creamy silk are nothing now
they're so last season, just passé.
Instead, he opens a display book where
a scarecrow in a man's waistcoat stares back,
her thin arm propped at the hip
above a long skirt of torn paper strips.
The new theme is The Bible, he says,
Old Testament, of course;
hand-printed, hand-shredded, only the best.

Or, for just a few thousand more
he'll knock you up this classic.
No one forgets a wedding when
the gown is made of fish,
their long bodies slung like blades around her waist
or if the dress is a shimmer of condom packets
that rustles like cellophane—
their edible contents saved for dessert
(surprise your guests).

You're thinking it would be cheaper
and more stylish
to cover yourself in masses of glue
and roll in some of the money you've scrimped,
but then he shows you the next picture
and you see that's been done too.

Now what's this at the back—
simple, sheer, and utterly you?
How much?

He frowns.
Fifty dollars, Madam.
It's a dry-cleaning bag.

Mixed Marriage

Her parents did not approve.
Mine made their point by moving to France.
One of us had too few tentacles
and breathed too much oxygen
but we worked our way through that.
These were minor problems.

I wore my best outfit.
She polished her antennae
and swung her hips in four dimensions.
I struggled with English syntax.
She spoke twelve languages
simultaneously.

The priest was reluctant.
It was a mixed faith wedding.
The reception was held in Dimboola.
We honeymooned on the moon
while I held my breath.
After all, love is about compromise.

We're hopeful for the future.
There's more tolerance these days.
Our kids will be multi-skilled,
bi-pedal, blue and many-gilled,
and if the neighbours are cruel,
we'll survive because she'll eat them alive.

The Wedding Present

It lies at the back of a drawer,
the third drawer of the chest
of drawers in the corner of the room
that catches the late afternoon light
in a soft diagonal of ivory
from the high window.

In there,
in the third drawer
behind the silk camisole
and the lace edge of some underwear
she's worn just twice,
it lies cool and matter of fact.

When her Uncle Guy was seventeen,
he bought it from a pawnbroker,
nudged the shop door and its small bell aside
to claim the shining form
that had winked at him from the window,
that had called him from across the street
to pull every coin and note he had
from his pockets.

Perhaps he fancied himself
a river-boat gambler
holding it snug in his palm,
the small but powerful part
of an equation he waited to see
spelt out before him
somewhere in the future,
real or imagined—
either way possible.

Her father hated it,
said that it went to his head,
Uncle Guy's head,
though his main complaint was
that it went to *his* head, her father's,
because of Uncle Guy's habit
when young and drunk
of waking her father
while holding the gun to the curve
of bone behind his ear
and talking about death for an hour,
about its pleasure and its inevitability.
Her father knew the circle of its barrel
firmly, intimately, against his skin
and the drunken whirl
of logic that kept it there.

Now, in the back of the drawer,
the small nickel-plated revolver
nestles against her underwear,
a gun neat as a baby's fist,
shiny as a champagne flute.
Its handle intricately carved from
mother of pearl
shows Lazarus rising.

Her father stole it from her uncle
when he was out drinking
and kept it in a sack in the garden shed
wrapped in hessian and laid next
to the new season's iris bulbs
until Uncle Guy began to forget
and her father began to grow as strange
as Uncle Guy had ever been
and one day,

her wedding day,
he presented it to her
as if a bunch of flowers,
smiling.

On its handle the figure is still looming
in subtle rainbow tints from its grave.
The gun is waiting,
cold and metallic,
and its purpose
instilled in those long nights
at her father's ear
is not forgotten.

In three weeks
she will pull out the drawer and
reach in there blind,
her hand, swimming around for a bra,
will connect for long enough
and the gun will finally fire
through the left cup,
through the back of the chest of drawers,
through the wall of the bedroom
and through the picture of her late father
and her late uncle
hanging in the next room.
One of them will suffer a flesh wound
at last.

Advice for the New Goth Bride

Nail your wedding dress to the wall
to remind you of your former, alien self.

Buy fireworks to celebrate special events
such as the anniversary of your first fight.

Train stacks of acrobatic cats
to distract neighbours from your escape.

Admire your shadow at midday.
It may be all that you have left.

If all else fails, practice boundless love
and other martial arts.

The Light

We were about
to live inside
a wedding cake marriage—
intricate
delicate,
a post-modern
deconstructed
angular
slab,
but that was
not for us.

It was an address of
too much sentiment—
floral
sweet as sugar,
far too dark in there
as we saw when the knife
and its sudden gash
let in the jilting light
and one of us fled.

Death Goes Wooing

I slick back an unruly lock of hair,
scuff my shoes on the trouser cuff
of my borrowed suit,
and enter the room smiling.
That first look is still a thrill.

Sometimes I'm rushed by circumstance
but I prefer a leisured approach,
wooing by degrees,
persuading with persistence
and natural charm.

My devotion is legendary.
I've lost count of my loves,
but it was never about numbers.
No, it's always been the chase,
despite the fact that
they all say Yes in the end.

A Frugal Proposal

A seed that's caught between my teeth,
a stone inside my shoe,
a gate that's squeaking in the wind,
all make me think of you.

Your cheeks aren't rosy apples,
no diamonds in your eyes,
you laugh like rusty hinges,
I don't care for your smile.

My little piece of cellophane,
my strand of broken string,
my recycled birthday card,
you're really quite the thing.

My only once-used alfoil,
my helpful scrap of stuff,
my hardly tarnished second-hand,
my almost good enough.

Your walk's a little awkward,
you snore each time you sleep,
your singing voice is woeful,
your ideas never deep.

But I've a fault or two myself,
as some have pointed out.
Could two wrongs make a right, perhaps?
Let us remove all doubt.

I must say I am hypnotised—
a wedding is the thing,
so, though it's pinched from a curtain rod,
please, darling, wear this ring.

Wedding Portrait: Chagall

You might say Blue as Deep Water,
or Emptiness, or Angels Dark as Coming Storms,
but all that foreboding dissolves,
useless in the face of this.

Nothing can be said after the fluid groom
and his bare bride, semi-transparent
and wrapped around each other,
drift away into a night sky.

The portrait sings sweet as honey in your ear.
Its devotions swim straight through you.
You hug it like the scripture of a rediscovered religion
that washes you in warm, engulfing certainty.

It is the sound of familiar music from before the war.
It is joy coming home with her name on its lips.
It is the face of the beloved as she stands at your door.
It is the swallowing and brilliant future that you walk into.

It is a man and a woman
giving themselves up to each other
regardless of protocols, customs, opinions, gravity.
The only poetry, their love.

All the Weddings

I am all the weddings—
the rapture,
the pageantry of her regal entry,
the stumbling speech,
the anxious bliss of the bridesmaid
and drunken best man
hastily fumbling their way out of
their clothing in a backroom,
fearful of discovery.

I am all the weddings—
the horrible griefs at the bustling
Afghan reception that is bombed
when mistaken for a terrorist gathering;
the child bride dolled-up like
a sideshow prize
staring into a sudden angry vacuum
that wants her more.

The too many too much
and not enoughness
of the whole tumbling circus
of uproar when forever now
simply will not hold its peace.

Sex and Love and Death

Rock stars spill from limousines.
Real stars fleck the blue-black skies,
little specks of ancient bling
winking out their long-dead light.

Cats asleep in circled fur
are breathing handbags, ears alert.
Their eyes closed to the day's concerns
offer more non sequiturs.

A bride ducks low her gauzy head—
fire-hiss whispers under breath.
Sheets as torn as a wedding dress.
Sex and love and sex and death.

Makeshift

Courting her,
I came to the used cereal packet that was her step
and carefully knocked twice,
my knuckles denting the cardboard door.

Houses there were made of fruit boxes
and old cans rolled flat and riveted for a roof—
bad work that let in sun and rain,
but the colours were stupidly pretty.

She called me inside.

I set my weeds in a jar on the milk-carton table
and glanced around the single room.
'What sort of bed is that,' I asked,
'and with three people already in it?'

'Be thankful,' she said.
Her thin arms threw the newspaper blanket open to me.
Fake pearls glistened on her breast.
'Come in quick, while they're still pretending to sleep.'

Bride of Frankenstein

I'm a simple mosaic
but not simple,
a patchwork of borrow and steal.

I would give my heart
if it were mine to give,
if you asked it of me.

What should I wear,
naked as the air,
but this scrawl of stitches?

They're the finest threads
but I don't care,
the crudest work would do.

I'm your betrothed,
the shadowed one
who wants the want in you.

The Rose Garden

After the Spring rain,
flamenco ruffles blossom on their racks.
The arbour erupts into soft chandeliers
and the rose garden's simply haute couture.
All the blooms toss up their skirts
in Folies Bergère,
their tousled heads a mad coiffure
of devil may care.
Such flim and flam,
such flounce and show,
such glam and sheer excess.
Their blowsy curves and pointed buds
stir the scented air.

Except in the corner of the yard
where the Mother of the Bride
is too uptight to stir
in her awful petalled hat,
disapproving perhaps
or simply lonely by herself.
While the rest shower pathways
with coloured scraps
slippery as painted lips,
she's prim and proper,
as reserved as the Queen of Sleep.

The others laze in afternoon's watery light
when we snip and clip,
bringing them in to vases and bowls
placed by drowsing windows.
Such opulence spoils us.
Their satin turbans shine like those

of sumptuous satraps,
royalty visiting our own home
where we're unsure of protocol.
Should we curtsy or bow
or dance for pleasure,
for the sheer hell of it?

Water

Even dry, a creek bed knows
the liquid heart beneath all things;
the constant river underground.
The world is an endless pour
between this place and that.

Love, like water, can't be held.
It is the vapour that we breathe,
our food and drink;
and patient love's a welcome rain,
our souls' replenishment.

They say we're nine-tenths water,
so place your hand in mine.
We'll be that constant river,
changing and the same.
We will flow together,
two streams joined as one.

Gathering

Dipping his fingers into her skull,
he ripples the water,
finds a spoonful of honey
a bundle of sticks
grated lemon peel
a pinch of dirt
a splinter in her finger
a stalk of lavender
a ball of string.

Here are the unread letters
and the wedding ring she lays
on her bedside table every night,
a tin-cup and whistle
the puzzle, the bits—
the world unravelling
in a jitterbug
St. Elmo's Fire.

But the angel at
the foot of her bed
is bored now—
watching the clock,
scratching his head
under a reggae hat
he stubs out his butt
and clicking his fingers
gathers her up.

Paper Doll

In this starchy light,
intense as wedding sheets' glare,
the bride is her own invention.
See her blooming.
She rises slowly,
unfolds as elegantly as a Japanese fan
but she is colourless fruit,
the husk of a scalded white wasp,
and her voice is no voice,
just the crackle of her own stiff fabrics
like spikes of radio waves flung into space—
the fierce static of absence.

Now she waits to kiss the one
who courted her under a paper moon,
her bleached lips as dry as her dress,
and here he comes.
In her thin hands she holds tight
a bright bouquet of scissors.

Dress Sense

Afterwards the wedding gown
is hung in a wardrobe,
a member of royalty
among the rustling lower class,
all those jealous silent commuters
where it's standing room only—
or else it's wrapped in tissue paper,
folded into a stiff lined box
and kept under the bed,
sleeping beneath the carnal river,
the tears of joy and last breaths.

A daughter may wear it
and a grand daughter
in a palimpsest of brides,
but eventually it will be consigned
to the old clothes basket
from which it might one day rise
to go princessing,
or to disguise a child in the costume
of a high-ranking official of the orient.
Lesser ones first float limply into op-shops
to be hauled out like pale fish
for fancy dress or scarecrow duty.

I am this odd one,
slung on a twist of wire
in the hen house,
queen of the muttering clutch

that settles to the night.
Some eye saw in me a perfect curtain
to fox and otherworld.
Now only the gully breeze fills me
and I will never be stepped from again,
never slump in a honeymoon sigh
of ivory silk and lace.
I am the reliquary past holiness,
garment of an exotic land,
sister to the brood,
dusty and white as my flock.

A Modern Vow

Repeat after me:
Will you, my beloved Patricia
   [the party of the first part]
knowing my great passion for you
   [subject to the conditions of the attached agreement]
consider me, your loving Patrick
   [the party of the second part]
to be your husband
   [as defined in sub-paragraph 3(g)]
sharing life's ups and downs
   [seasonally adjusted]
and forsaking all others
   [as far as clause 8 requires]
so long as we both shall live *
   [according to Statute 12 of
    the Medical Assistance Act of 2003]?

If so,
please click in the box,
enter credit card details
and hit Send #

   no warranty, expressed or implied, is given
   # the security of this transaction is not guaranteed

On Second Thought

On second thought
the suitor stays at home.
He sends his suit instead.
A hundred-dollar hire,
it knows the haunts
of doubts and vows,
arrives in time
to meet the empty gown
that is fashionably late.

A perfect match
   brideless
   groomless
they
honeymoon in
a wardrobe near you.

Dachau

You'll rise when ready,
dust off the years,
collect your clothing from the heap
and dress without embarrassment
among the naked crowd.

You'll find your watch easily among
the thousands sprawled on the tables
and your ring will be an obvious circle
in the first wooden box you choose
from all those stacked against the wall.

Pick up the brown suitcase
from the corner where it was thrown,
your tag still on the broken handle,
then consult the list on the desk
to uncross your name
and all that will be left
will be to walk the yard
to board the train home.

The sun will be shining
as you wait by the track,
the grass swooning in the wind
and conversations will begin
of trivial things—
which curtains to put in the kitchen,
what dress to wear to a cousin's wedding,
where to plant the roses.

The Love Songs of Lawyers

The love songs of lawyers
are like their dancing,
slow as cows walking home,
a cumbersome poise.
Romance is a contract in draft.
They court each other with lyrics
wherein the party of the first part
woos the party of the second,
though beyond the riders,
and clauses and heretofores,
I can still hear the faint sound
of a charmed language.

When I sense their heartfelt ballads
I think of whales calling across the sea floor.
Even retuned to my frequency,
it's a strange dialect I'll never truly know
that aches with lugubrious majesty.

Out there in the moonlight
their strange calls linger.
Terms pitched above ears' normal range
hang in the thin air
like the mating cries of bats—
a para-legal calling for a pal,
a barrister cooing.
The shy courtships sound
down the miles of cases held over
for adjournments of the heart.

The Groom

the groom is
made of twigs
sticks and bits
of dry leaves

voodoo doll
black-cat bone
ju-ju
dead wood

but a little spit
a bead of blood
wets the tiny
pulsing heart

dark berry eyes open
twiggy fingers twitch
a bride out there somewhere
he feels that needy itch

The Bride We Pass

The bride we pass on the side of the street,
that white figure
walking the footpath with her head erect
and long train trailing in the dirt,
has popped out to the shop for some smokes, I say,
or is breaking in the dress for a friend.

As she dwindles in our mirrors,
you pause at my joke, then say,
No, she has told the driver of the wedding car
'Just stop here,'
suddenly afraid of the stranger who wears the gown
and the other one who will take it off.

And though your hand still rests on my leg
as I drive, we don't talk again
the whole way home.

Little Murders

When she walks the aisle
she's sexless and pure sex
in a crown of lavender and cloves,
unwanting and wanted,
saint and seductress.
Her veil's made of spun sugar,
a glistening confection,
a light snack for someone
already licking his lips.

She glides toward the altar
like a fairy princess.
Her bridal gown of bees' wings
took a million little murders,
more or less.

Not seeing in the future,
half a life and miles away,
a house in weeds and rust,
the smell of sulphur in the air
before the days of rain,
the raw spines of nettles on the sink,
a slack-string guitar
and a wire-door closing.

The Reluctant Bride

I was promised, custom said
but when they came
I found an attic box
just big enough to hide me
until they had all left,
then I fled over rooftops
clambered down a walnut tree—
the back-fences, roads, fields,
the next town, a train, a ship.
Days and breathless days
I ran and ran.

I slept in cellars and under stars.
I slept in frosted orchards
by the glow of smudge-pots.
I changed my name and dyed my hair.
I learnt a new language.
I dressed as a boy.
I wore a tattoo.
I worked on road-gangs.
I traded skins
that made me three fortunes I lost,
then I set out beyond the camps and houses,
beyond the world of man.

There I ate wild fruit and raided nests.
I fought with lions and a mad moon—
then, where skies turn a roiling mass of blue,
where birds live underground and fish in air,
I stopped running.
I built a house from mud and sticks,
bred honeybees,
grew pears
and stayed.

Six years safe
and here he comes again,
his step less sure
and without his clamouring entourage
but I know that grin.
I'll stand at the doorway
in my own rough finery to greet him
and this time
maybe
I will
just say No.

Speak Now

it is a wedding with
    no bride
a wedding with
    no groom

the jilted ex comes
    without a gift
and sits in the back row
    picking his nails

the nervous priest
    offers a little joke
the ex permits himself
    a little smile

a bee at the stained glass
    butts its furry head
there is so much time
    to wait in

across winter skies
    light sleeps on the wreckage
across the suburbs
    a woman enters an empty house

a broken guitar
    a letter never sent
burnt photographs of weddings
    without a bride or groom

if anyone here objects
    speak now

The Happy Couple

after Imogen's painting

You and I can only stare forwards
from our wedding portrait here
though I still sense you next to me
when I strain my eyes to the side,
this bride of mine I can't quite face.
Your hands are the shoots of two branches,
your hair a river of wheat.
I know you are smiling like me.

The sky is half blue and clear
of everything but itself,
the rest filled with clouds and rainbows
and crowds of singing bees.
I stand in bright grasses
where I had waited for you,
till a brush filled you in,
letting it all revolve above me,
sinking my feet into the papery earth.

Once my hair was spiky short,
a jagged crown with a halo of fire.
Then my daughter painted it long and wild,
coloured and tied with wiry bows
as it fell down to the ground
like a ravelling cape behind me.
I think I see birds in there too.

Off to our left is a house with a chimney
and a tree in the yard
where a swing is hanging.
Perhaps it is where we will stay,
but for now it is just out of reach
and we live where we both stand unmoving,
basking in this yellow wash of light—
before night comes quickly,
sudden as the closing of a book.

Clowns in Love

Behind the pratfalls and the bright red nose,
you'd like to think there is someone like us
when they're off duty,
as ordinary as an executioner eating dinner,
but the truth is that
even in bed there's still that lunatic smile,
the slapstick and tears
where the make-up smears
and the body's awkward language of sex
flicks between pictures of cartoon excess.

They prank to hide grief.
Romeo with rubber knife and a fizzing mug,
Othello with outsize hankie
playing tragedy for laughs,
and no passion is too big for mime.
Even if their big shoes get in the way,
their fat hearts still beat on their sleeves.

It's a courtship with animal balloons
and a rain of glitter,
with flapping arms and Look out behind you!
until she says Yes.
Then nothing is done by halves—
the wedding ring's really a water pistol,
the bouquet explodes into scarves,
the in-laws are drowned in confetti
as the couple departs in a pedal car,
throwing custard pies at each other.
True love, they know, is no joke.

The Floating Bride

The thin red line of a thousand-acre seasonal burn
turns stubble into a wide, white train of smoke
that hangs above the autumn horizon for hours
before dissipating in a starless bone-chill night.

Morning sun draws gauzy mist from the gully
and the quiet run of Ferris Creek.
In its deepest pool, Bridget's gowned body
is nudged by a school of small fish
that are the colour of her staring eyes.
No one is missing her yet.

53

Analogue

The World According to Scissors

You might say Siamesed predator
of those less strong.
I am we, the one in two,
who comes unhinged to work.
I open mouth or legs, you choose,
and eat the world away.

Though I do love paper.
I remain dubious of stone.
That relationship is vexed.
I whet myself with pleasure there
but stone is betrayer, blunting.
Stone does not love me.

I am the passive one really,
the kept pet stuck in drawer or jar.
You are most to blame,
with your finger in each socket
and your voracious appetite
for cruelty so transparent.

Skywriting

Cyrillics written onto blue
in brilliant uncertainty,
clouds' arguments are airy, indecisive.
Their beautiful, garrulous nonsense

is constantly erased and painted over.
Who are they telling, and what,
unconcerned by us who fail to read the signs
before they evaporate?

Then rain catches us and we see
the message was never meant for you or me
but the very slow talker
biding its time beneath our feet.

What does it say, the sky to the ground?
We stand like eavesdroppers listening in
on its public and intimate whisperings.
What on earth does it need to say?

Thunder, Lightning

I was distant thunder, lightning.
I was an old tune on the radio.
I was the purr of rain on the window.
I was everywhere, though unimportant.

You said it was only a dream,
that all we lived was illusion,
and not really living,
so, yes, nothing mattered.

I shaved my head.
I gave away my possessions
but I was doing something wrong,
still found that I belonged.

A light in the sky
wanted clouds and birds
and approaching rain,
and someone to watch it.

It was me.
I was the solo, the choir,
the end of the song and story,
every kind of junk and glory.

The Simplified Book of Dreams

Dreaming of finding a coin on the path
means you will be kind to a stranger.
Dreaming of being naked in public
means you will feel a hole in your pocket.

Dreaming that a cat tells you jokes in Russian,
that your car has no steering wheel,
that you climb an endless flight of stairs,
that stars in the river spell her name backwards,
that a door in your house reveals a room never seen before,
that you find a book glued fast to the ground,
means you should stop writing this poem right now
and go straight back to sleep.

The Missing Years

Where did he go after
he stepped from the public gaze?
What did he do in those missing years?
There are no photographs.
He did not write letters
or make new friends.

Some sources say
that for three years he ran a shop
selling postcards in New Zealand,
that he sailed across Lake Carver
in a small boat made of old inner tubes,
and married a Finnish musician.

There are unconfirmed reports of
a stint collecting hubcaps
for an avant garde gallery,
that he worked as a booking clerk
for a shipping firm and
wrote a novel he then burned.

Whatever he did,
when he was found by his biggest fan
and shot twice in the chest,
as he lay dying on the ground,
whose life passed before his eyes
when he simply said, 'Done'?

St Bart's

I   St Bart's Gallery

> *I am the way and the truth and the life*
>
> John 14:6

I walk from the street into an inverted boat.
The church is beached,
like a fisherman's dinghy upturned on the shore,
jammed between houses
where the tide is never in.
It's no Noah's ark. The sharp V
of its keel pulls plank and plank together
like fingers touching high above me.
Maybe Christ's in dry dock.

I sit and wait and watch the watching gallery of saints.
Lit like comic superheroes in their frames,
they want my little darkness
to shine all their good deeds upon.
The hull above is lapped by the day's flammable blue,
light that comes from Heaven via the suburbs,
and when they sleep, it is under
the moth-holed cloth of night's dark.

I have been in other craft like this,
vessels in a scattered fleet
that sail by an awkward chart.
In a church some years ago
the inside was lit by the ordinary,
windows of burnt barley sugar
stealing light to show a woman
hanging shirts on a backyard line,
a couple flinging up a sheet to make a bed,

children playing in a yard,
and in the largest was a couch-bound family
washed in the pale blue rinse of a TV set
just outside the frame.
Those windows stained by the daily,
the simple ebb and flow of ritual.
I knew they said the real and felt at home.

This church today is more the norm,
with its blazoned characters like Tarot cards.
The necessary knight, St George,
is armoured in faith's finery,
gazing blankly, bored as a rock star
dazzled by another camera flash,
he's doped on sunshine.
St Alban in bright fancy dress, a Roman soldier's garb,
is haughty as a fashion model stalled on a runway.
The pair of Christs seem wraithlike, tired.
One's a wan Light of the World,
lost and uncertain, with lamp in hand;
the other's looking skyward, his mind on going home.

Best is the nativity in open air,
Mary with Baby J. in arms.
He wears a lifebuoy halo of red and white,
and she a round and luminous disk,
like a hat for going to the races.
Her face has a childcare worker's patient calm,
but at her bare feet is a stream with two arched fish
that seem in pain. This small detail,
marginalia on an illustrated manuscript,
offers the rawest feeling.
I want to ask why it hurts them so.
A foreseen grief?
Mary knows but will not tell.

II Church Music

i. Chorus
We are drab and glorious,
plain and beautiful as air.
Outside's kerosene blue vapour
breathes through us all day.

We are breakable and tense,
stiff cartoon go-betweens.
We're a strange family in
the weirdest family album.

We're cardboard cut-outs
living on borrowed light,
frozen medieval glossies,
the slowest of slide shows.

Yet when you look away from us
we flicker in the corner of your eye,
ghosts tugged by a solar gust
that live and live and live.

ii. Solo
By day I am all Disney,
gaudy as Gaudi in my glad rags,
a vivid test pattern portrait.

At night the light creeps back out
through my brittle skin
to the speckled sky.

It's like sleep.
It's like dreaming.
There's no stiller life than mine.

III. Church Going

> *... the place was not worth stopping for.*
> *Yet stop I did*
>> Philip Larkin, 'Church Going'

As odd as a God kennel,
steep-roofed and timbered,
His house is eccentric.
Someone had a sense of humour building this.

Within the burning light of brass
and gloss of polished pew,
some other kind of glow licks at these surfaces.
Irreverent or not, I'd say a whisky hue.

And then those faces looking down
from the main stained window
like a mighty choir in full regalia,
an overdose of technicolour.

It's a barn, too big,
not intimate at all until my sitting finds me
thinking I'm a church inside a church.
I feel reluctant then to go, but leave.

Stepping back outside I feel
not a world that's turned about,
or upside down or inside out,
but a difference more subtle.

God was not at home today.
I'll visit more if he stays away.

When We Shone

Before the storm
we were the calm that spoke
of rust and rain, fallen animals.

We were as precious as jewels
and stories of gone times,
never having to sing the truth.

When we shone,
our glow lit whole suburbs,
everything bathed in our presence.

We used to know
what we were talking about
until the metaphors and puzzles.

Now we're bones and the music
of former times,
but still beautiful.

The headlines have faded.
Our light has dimmed,
as it must for us to rest,
blessed with forgetfulness,
released into darkness at last.

Acts of Grace

1.

Our leaders spoke in riddles
folded inside futile metaphors.
They washed their hands with regrets
and packed their bags for escape.

We hoarded, scouring store shelves
before our houses sloughed off power.
Darkness and hunger sang
a bitter duet across the land.

Who knows the music of us anymore?
Closing churches and cities was no cure.
We slaughtered helpless creatures,
became their holocaust and sour requiem.

Pestilence played no favourites.
Its brutal blessing was freely given;
just a few of us surviving
through potions or puzzling grace.

2.

No masks could filter the angry truth.
No amount of spending quell
our fear of its approach
or redeem our masters' failure.

Travellers we'd turned from our doors
in the worst days of contagion
welcomed us into their multitudes
at sprawling riverside camps.

They saw no enemies,
held no blame even for thieves,
shared prayers and offered shelter,
mercies for the faithless or weak.

First-world hermits together,
we held tight as if to cave-fires,
while the scourge stalked the frail,
gathered them in its cruel embrace.

3.

Since that terrible cleansing has ebbed,
the songs of bees are golden;
honey and ashes lie in the heaped bones
of our beloved lost.

Now we live upon our knees.
It is all we can do.
Empty streets can't speak our names.
Scavenging angels look away.

So, I ask you, God,
do you still know my face?
My dearest are all dead.
How can I still sing your praises?

But I will, un-alone and grateful,
part of a larger tribe.
I am ready for this rough new Eden,
its bright language of grief and hope.

Storm

The house is a shattering of wind
and fleeing birds,
its windows shaking in their frames
played like drums in hail-shot rain
as if on the brink of collapse.

How fragile we are in here,
all night paper-thin and fearful,
startled by thundered light
that fractures our brief bravado at a whim
with camera flashes of stunned faces.

A calm will come, we know,
but there are hours to go
and we could drown in these rooms,
insignificant as the electric air.

Piano Mouth

The song in my head
is off-key and beautiful.
She plays every note wrong
but I dance all the same.

We know each step
and together mistake our way
through to the end,
incorrectly perfect,
to encore after encore
that we always demand.

Ghosts

We skeletons, twitchysticks.
We rockets, flare and pulse.
We pretty, flammable glam.
We dancers, rickety steps.
We sweethearts, photo photo.
We phosphor, brighter light.
We Houdini, escape-key kisses.
We quicksilver, broken mirror leak.
We tinder, flash fire and gone.
We shadow, passing cloud over.
We floodway, sweep and storm-wash.
We sky-riders, swoop wind and glide.
We stupid, know less than.
We history.   Forget us soon.

Epilogue

As he lay dying,
a well-lived life flashed before his eyes,
but not his own.
Too late to ask for his money back.
No choice but to watch the show.

A blitzing synopsis of past attractions,
it included a tall woman
rising from a bath,
whom he might have loved
if he was someone else,
then two small children holding hands
in a garden more tropical than his
and, in the background, the flare
of a harbour lit by sails.

He wondered, as the show unravelled,
who had mixed up the reels?
Whose life was this?
The one he missed
through some turn in fate?
And who was watching his?
Where was Sharon
and her delicious smile?
Who'd got her and the kids
on their own final screen?
Who got his famous jetty dive
and his first bike ride?

No raincheck now,
just a blur of dimming lights,
the curtain's hiss
and darkness.

The Waking Child

He wakes four times this night.
The first finds him out of bed,
wedged between mattress and wall.
I lift him up and lie beside
until his breath relaxes,
listening to passing trains,
the rumbling trucks and silences
before retreating to my own bed.

His last cry launches me awake,
an automaton to duty flung,
but he's asleep, unstirred, eyes closed,
and I have hours to count
the street-sweeping machine's
trip up and down the road,
the single ambulance siren keening the night,
the interstate hauliers' sighing brakes
and all the reasons to be thankful
for three-year-olds who wake.

What grave things I have to contemplate,
what great treasures to keep,
what sweet and private joys
before I lose them in my own sleep,
the roads awash with the constant freight
of the unlit hours' precious cargoes.

Taking Care

This song is not for you.
Its spark kept in a box
will not spill light in your presence.
Its wonderful voice stored darkly now
is gathering animal strength
towards eventual release,
but only when you are long gone.

This song is not for you.
Its aural acrobatics will jolt others
to suddenly gasp
but you will not hear them.
You might even see its glow on the horizon
as that of a city beyond a ridge,
one you cannot visit.

This is just to ask that you hold fast.
Right now you are simply required
to pass it on when told.
For this caretaking, this kindness,
there is another song coming
in which you will be wing and claw
and the splintering fireworks of stars.

Chainsaw Blues

Several houses away
sometime after two a.m.,
the unmistakable whine
plays rough and intermittently.

Maybe someone sleepless and cold
needing more firewood
and careless of his neighbours'
long wakefulness.

Morning shows the whole yard there
sawn to smithereens—
trees, rose bushes, letterbox, shrubs,
all in ragged piles.

Deserted in the middle of this debris
is the bright yellow machine,
its stilled teeth still smiling—
the drunken divorce settlement.

True Story

It's not in the rain of bombs,
streets of ruined houses
or the grief.

It's not in the soldier's faces,
the scattered bodies
or the heat.

It's not in protest marches,
the gassing of tribes
or aid withheld.

It's not in our conversations,
a poem
or troubled dreams.

The true story of the war
is in the memoirs
of the politicians and the generals
who were on our side, not yours.
Ask them if it isn't so.

War Music

They all know the tune too well,
those thousands who flounder awake
in the thrall of night-time thunder
and can't find darkness's sweet arms again.
Their best mate's throat fills with blood.
The whine of bullets still goes on.
A dull percussion tears to shreds
their years of safety, that barbed survival.

While families sleep inside, content,
old soldiers thrash a sleep-out cot to bits
in roaring silence, waiting for
magpies' dawn chorus to sing relief,
a kind of blessing life might bring
to those who danced with death.

The Contagion Years: A Blessing

In this long quarantine
there is at least one blessing—
the small prayer still to be had
on my knees in an unkempt garden
with dirt under my nails,
posing questions with soil and plants
about the future and its fruit.

While in this house arrest, I dig for hope,
down into the under-me,
the earth my forebears worked
in faith or doubt—
those past, those buried,
all the unrisen,
and wonder where I am.

The same sun shines above me.
The same sparrows congregate
to see the fertile dirt disturbed
in this small church beneath my hands
with its chance of bugs and worms
while I think seeds, a coming season,
and what I might be then, if I still am at all.

The Internet is Full

The internet is full.
We can't even send you an error message
to break the sad news.
You'll just have to curse your computer,
your ISP, your server, your god;
anyone who might solve your exile
or at least seem worthy of blame.

When your screen plays dumb
and an indifferent sun rises over your isolation;
after your pleading for contact becomes soft bleating
down the phone line to countless
Your Business is Important to Us automatons,
the seven stages of grief will take turns to
wear you like a store dummy's costume,
each driving you toward numbness.

You might eventually go outside
to rail against the night sky,
the bright white dots of distant light
still uttering their usual cold greeting.
Some messages cover vast distances
and empty space for aeons to say nothing
that we can understand.

Fullness. Emptiness.
Sometimes the same.

Listening

'You talked,' she said,
while she drove that morning,
gripping and releasing the wheel
as if uncertain what to add.
'You talked in your sleep.
You said the cats' names
like you were calling
them to dinner.'

I almost said I don't talk in my sleep,
but how would I prove it?
I worried what she'd say next.
A woman's name, real or not?
Something else uttered from the brain's deep
or that floating dream world?
Either way already condemned
by my pre-emptive sense of guilt.

The Woman on Fire

The woman on fire
consulted the bones of her wrist
as if checking a watch,
laid her dress down on the bed
and stepped into the garden
knowing that after her sorrow
the choice would be easy,
that the tin and match,
the flames between the roses and
the scorching leaves,
would fold into themselves
and nothingness.

Don't make it mysterious.
This is not about you.
The woman on fire
doesn't want to know about you.
Her boundaries found wanting,
she lets them go,
that imperative of body/not body
loosened for good,
her edges will turn vaporous.
It is simpler.
You can give up possessions;
even the body.
Sometimes most easily the body.

Don't talk of angels
or states of grace.
She will forsake the house of self,
going out of the pride of things.
There is the long exhalation,

the body only a kind of theory
that she will deconstruct,
abandoning its tenacious meanings—
the first boy's hand on her thigh,
a swim at midnight,
the clamouring list of memories,
the body's arrogance,
its claims,
its joys and complaints.
A child at the centre of a child
refusing to be earth quite yet
but committed to go.
A brief luminescence,
but it is not for that,
the afterwards;
the end of claims,
of being owned.
She waits in the fire
for what lies beyond waiting.

Heat Wave

Only I am awake.
The lightning has retreated over the ridge
with its attendant barks of thunder.
The heat is finally going out of the night.
My daughters upstairs had the worst of it,
finally falling asleep to crickets and distant cars,
the patter of intermittent rain.

The cat makes a cat's space on our bed,
the freight train plays its long knife-sharpening
song of rumble and squeal,
and then it is silence—
broken suddenly by our eldest talking in her sleep,
'Where shall I be?' she calls,
'Where shall I be?'

We are all here—
like dozing fish at the bottom of a pond,
heavy as the stillness of summer air
pressing us down,
but where shall we be?

The Radiants Speak

We are eating pearls and diamonds,
tigers lounging at our feet,
the plains sprawl below us,
all our kingdoms dreamt and real.

Knuckled moon above
in a sky pockmarked with stars.
You don't need shadows
when you own the light.

We have heard the dead singing
all their beautiful mistakes.
They outnumber us
but we are more wonderful.

In the room that God left empty,
the poets still debate space and line.
We're not holding our breath
for any break-through soon.

Keep sending flowers and sacrifices.
We'll descend among you one day,
aglow with difference and attitude,
handing out some kind of useless mercy.

Then We Jumped

The details are always the same—
the ones you're interested in.
Just tick that box and forget it.

You weren't up there
with that choice crooning its woo
in your own yes/no/maybe head.

It's just physics in the end.
The clouds were indifferent
and we would soon be everywhere.

Nothing Zen to us then,
soon to be as thin as the charms
of the falling air we'd embrace

before rising among dead stars,
tomorrow's weather always
waiting below us,

drowning in the view of you
falling up towards us
so solemnly.

Rations

They bring in light by the truckload—
loud, heaving vehicles that
move through the suburbs
in guarded convoys at night.

We queue for our ration.
No special pleading,
no favours allowed,
all equal, they say,
but the officials' houses
blaze lavishly.

We hoard our meagre portion,
learn to move by touch,
recall when light was squandered
in the days of abundance.

The moon is our lantern now.
No poetry left in that.
We can't capture it beyond our songs
about trucks and blackened houses,
ourselves reflected in other eyes
lit by bitter garden fires.

The Art of Nations

We make abandoned buildings.
Some of them take years—
the right neglect,
the exact rate of decay.

Soon we will graduate to cities.
One of yours
has been selected
for perfect ruin.

Our patrons are generous.
Even their armies
have your interests at heart.
They will guide you in your leaving.

Sometimes you will be able to
take more with you than your lives.

Flowers

In the valley of the mass executions,
flowers grow.
Always have, always will.

After/Life

What was speak
when it had my mouth
before other home?

Up comes curious.
Little say it says,
unmurder me.

What was I said?
Sweetheart?
Sweet word?

Now tide sleeps us,
sweet-talking
our voices like water.

You hear it together
but we are more
gone now than ever.

At World's End

It might as well be a party
with picnics in every park,
the shops are open to everyone
for cashless carry,
for free takeaway.
I called in sick, reckless
of my perfect attendance record
just to hear no one answer the phone.
I've taken up smoking
and whistling in the streets.

I tell you what I really think about you,
which is that no angel could match you.
We slough off gods,
sing only to each other,
and when the final gloom or brilliance
announces sleep,
whose hands will we hold
if not the children's,
lifting them into our arms
and not telling them why?

No one packs their bags.
Electricity fails.
Phones no longer work,
except for selfies.
The only possible goodbyes are to
those close by,
and then we'll be wind and dust
as we were before.

I hear the song on the horizon
and it is not rapturous.
It is too late coming, too soon,
and after the brilliance, only oblivion.
But first you have a moment
to chalk a line of poetry
on the ground
and draw a bird after it.

About the Author

Steve Evans has taught literature and creative writing in the community and in universities, most recently as the Director of the Creative Writing Program at Flinders University. After the award-winning first poetry collection, *Edison Doesn't Invent the Car*, he went on to win further prizes, including the Queensland Premier's Poetry Prize and a Barbara Hanrahan Fellowship, and has been shortlisted for several national and international awards. He has written and edited twenty-one other titles besides *The Crow on the Cross*, his tenth collection of poetry.

Other works by Steve Evans

Poetry
Adult Fiction
Algebra
Animal Instincts
Bonetown
Edison Doesn't Invent the Car
Luminous Fruit
Taking Shape
Unearthly Pleasures (*published by in case of emergency press*)
Useful Translations

Fiction
Easy Money and Other Stories

Non-fiction
Balancing Act: The Creative Writing Pathway to Understanding Accounting (*with Lee Parker*)
Best of Friends: the first 30 years of the Friendly Street Poets (*with Kate Deller-Evans*)
Lift Off! an introductory course in creative writing (*with Kate Deller-Evans*)

As Editor
Another Universe (*with Kate Deller-Evans*)
Corridors: Words on the Ward (*with Kate Deller-Evans*)
Lament – Michèle St Yves
New Poets 20
New Poets 21
New Poets 22
Ochre 10
synonym for sobriety – Ben Adams

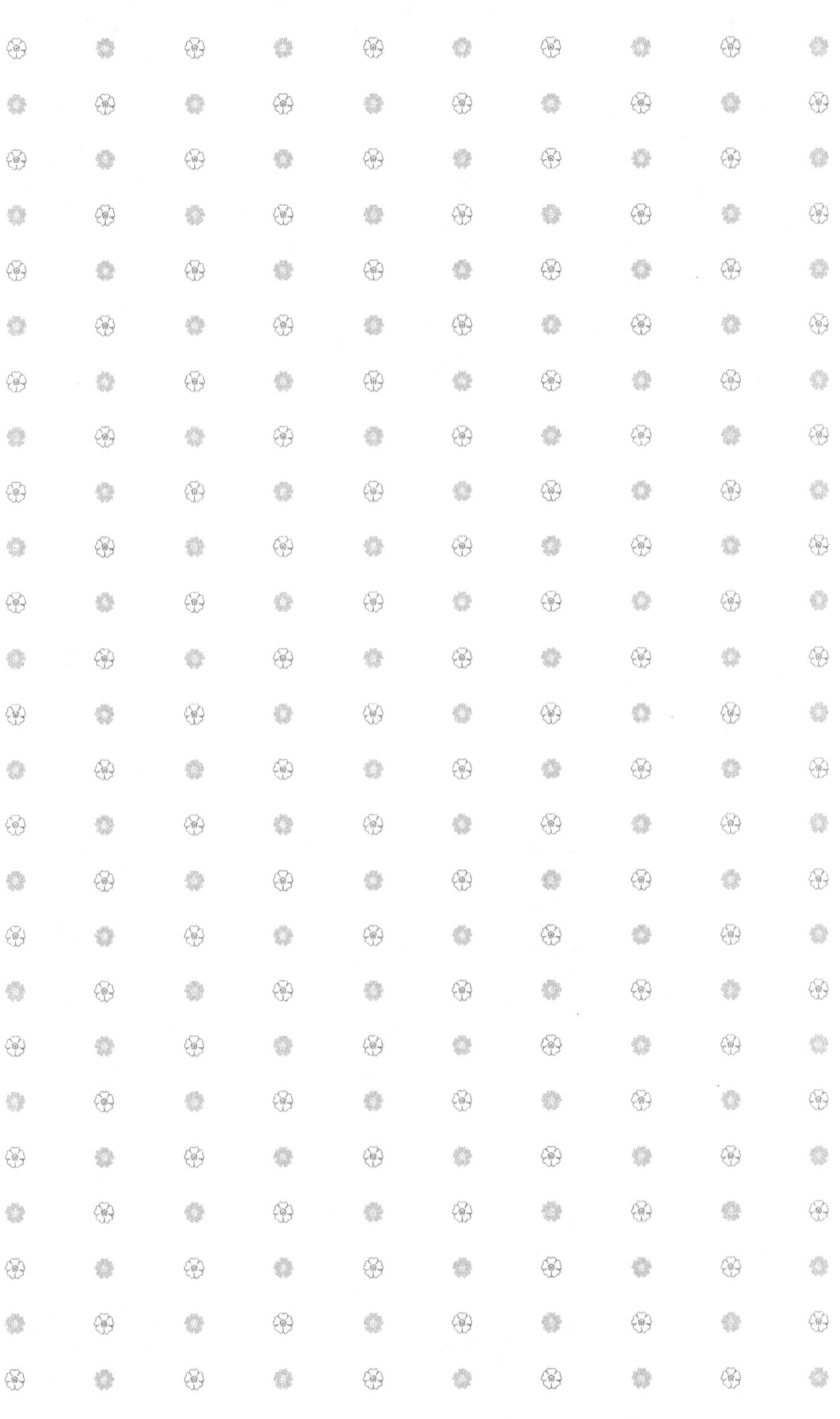

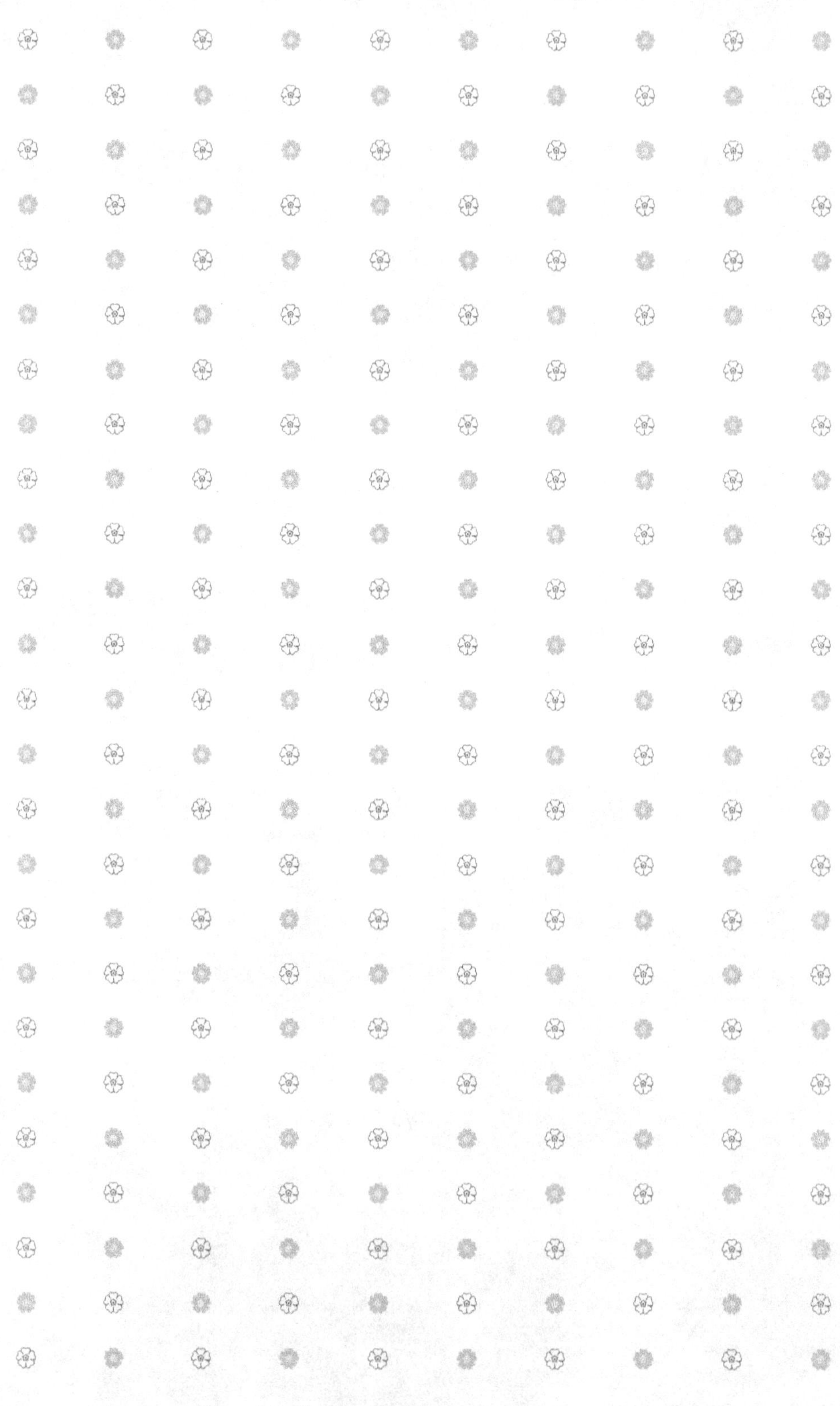